Trading Harmonic

Madelyn Price

Madelyn Price

Copyright Page

Copyright Holder: © 2024, Andrea Jimenez
Year: 2024
Author: © 2024, Madelyn Price

Legal and Copyright Information

First edition
All Rights Reserved

Index

Introduction to Harmonic Trading

Trading is an activity that many people associate with charts, numbers, and fast market movements. However, what few people know is that beyond technical and fundamental analysis, there is a much deeper dimension to the world of trading: the spiritual connection with the market. In this book, we are going to explore a different way of looking at trading, a way that seeks to align with the invisible forces that guide market movements, but that are also deeply linked to our mind, our emotions, and our spirit. We will call this approach "Harmonic Trading."

Harmonic Trading is based on the idea that the market is not just a series of cold, mechanical transactions. The market is a living entity, constantly changing and moving, and as such, it requires that we approach it with a clear mind, a calm heart, and a deep connection to our inner self. It is not just about following patterns or trends; it is about getting in tune with the natural flow of the market. This may sound a bit abstract, but it is a reality that many traders experience after years of trading. It is as if, after much practice and patience, you can "feel" the market, anticipating movements not only with data, but with well-honed intuition.

But to get to that point, we need more than just technical knowledge. We need to train our mind and spirit. In the modern world, trading has become a high-intensity activity. Markets move at breakneck speed, and emotions like fear, greed, and anxiety can easily take over any trader, leading them to make rash decisions that end in losses. This is where the Harmonious Approach comes into play. Through this method, we will learn to calm our mind, manage our emotions, and prepare to face trading sessions with unwavering calm, no matter what is happening in the market.

One of the foundations of Harmonic Trading is the understanding that, just like in nature, everything in the market follows a cycle. There are times of ups and times of downs, just as the tides rise and fall. Learning to embrace these cycles, rather than resist them, is critical to successful trading. We cannot control the market, but we can control our response to it. And to do this, we need to be at peace with ourselves. Only when our mind is calm and focused can we clearly see the opportunities that are presented to us.

This book will guide you through practices and concepts that go beyond typical trading strategies. We will explore the importance of meditation, visualization, and emotional self-control. We will see how these tools not only help us improve our skills as traders, but also grow as people. Because, at the end of the day, trading is not just a money game; it is a personal journey. Every trade we make offers us the opportunity to learn something new about ourselves: our strengths, our weaknesses, and above all, our ability to remain calm in the midst of chaos.

Connecting harmoniously with the market doesn't mean you'll never lose again. Trading is inherently risky, and losses are part of the process. What changes with this approach, however, is our perspective. Instead of seeing a loss as a failure, we can see it as a lesson. Instead of despairing when the market moves against us, we can remain calm knowing that it's all part of a larger cycle, and that new opportunities will arise if we remain open-minded and patient.

The goal of this book is to help you develop a healthier, more balanced relationship with trading. We will teach you to trade from a place of calm and mental clarity, rather than being swept away by panic or euphoria. You don't need to be a market guru to be successful; you just need to be at peace with yourself. And when you achieve that, trading the market becomes a completely different experience, almost like a dance where you move to the rhythm of the market, rather than fighting against it.

Harmonic Trading is not just a technique, it is a philosophy. It is a way of seeing the market and yourself as part of a greater whole. It is understanding that your success in trading is directly related to your ability to remain calm, focused, and in inner harmony. Throughout this book, you will discover how you can apply these principles in your daily trading, and how, by doing so, you will not only improve your results, but also your overall quality of life.

This is a journey of self-discovery and personal growth as much as it is of improving your skills as a trader. I hope that by the end of this book, you will not only be more successful in your trading, but also find greater inner peace, a deeper connection with yourself and the market. Because when we operate from a place of harmony, the results are not only better, but also more satisfying.

The Natural Flow of the Market

The financial market, in many ways, behaves like a way of life. Like a river, it flows constantly, sometimes with calm waters and other times with strong, fast currents. If we try to fight against that current, we quickly become exhausted and, more often than not, lose the battle. However, if we learn to navigate with the flow of the river, we can go much further with less effort. This idea of going with the flow of the market is key for any trader looking to be successful in the long term, and it is the essence of the "natural flow of the market."

The market has its own rhythms and cycles, much like the cycles of nature. Just as there are seasons of the year, the market also has times of expansion and contraction, growth and decline. These cycles are not always exactly predictable, but if we look closely, we can notice repeated patterns. A good trader is like an observer of nature, patient and attentive, who knows when the right time to act is. Understanding and accepting that the market follows its own course, and not ours, is one of the greatest learnings we can have.

One of the biggest mistakes traders, especially new ones, make is trying to impose their will on the market. This approach rarely works. Trying to force a trade or ignoring the signals the market is giving us only leads to losses and frustration. It's like trying to swim upstream; no matter how hard you try, the current is much stronger than you. That's why it's important to learn to read the market with an open and flexible mind. When we try to impose our will, we become rigid, and the market, which is dynamic and changing, does not respond well to that rigidity.

But how can we learn to go with the flow of the market? The first thing is to develop the ability to observe without reacting immediately. Often, when we see an opportunity or a sudden movement in prices, our first reaction is to rush into action. However, harmonious trading teaches us that patience is a key virtue. Instead of reacting to the first change we see, we should take a moment to breathe, observe, and feel what is happening. Just like a surfer waits for the right wave to ride, we too should wait for the ideal moment to enter the market.

Another important thing to recognize is that, just like the weather, the market has "seasons." There are times of high volatility, where prices rise and fall rapidly, and there are times of calm, where movements are slower and more predictable. Both phases are a natural part of the market flow, and we cannot expect to always be in one or the other. A good trader learns to adapt to these different phases, adjusting his strategy and approach according to the market environment at the time. Just as we would not wear the same clothes in winter as we would in summer, we should not trade the same way in different market conditions.

A key aspect of going with the flow is also learning to accept the unexpected. In nature, not everything is predictable. There can be sudden storms, changes in the weather, or unexpected events. The same is true in the market. Sometimes, everything seems to indicate that prices will continue to rise, but suddenly there is an unexpected drop. If we hold on too tightly to our expectations or our predictions, we can get caught up in that surprise and make mistakes out of fear or frustration. However, if we adopt a more fluid mindset, we understand that these events are part of the natural cycle of the market and we should not fear them, but rather adapt to them.

Going with the flow of the market doesn't mean we have to be passive. It's not about simply accepting everything that happens without taking action. On the contrary, it's about acting at the right time, with a clear mind and without forcing things. When a river flows strongly, a good navigator doesn't try to stop, but uses that energy to his advantage to move forward. Similarly, as traders, we must learn to use the market's movements, both bullish and bearish, to our advantage. This requires practice, but above all it requires a mind that is in tune with what the market is telling us.

One of the best ways to develop this ability to flow with the market is through the practice of mindfulness. By staying present in each moment and in each trade, we can more clearly observe what is happening, without being swept away by our emotions or impulses. Instead of reacting to every little fluctuation, we learn to make decisions from a place of calm and focus. Not only does this improve our accuracy as traders, but it also helps us stay emotionally balanced, avoiding the burnout and stress that often accompanies trading.

In short, the natural flow of the market is something that all traders must learn to respect. The market has its own rhythm, its own cycles, and our task is not to control it, but to learn to move with it. When we stop fighting the market and start flowing with it, trading becomes less stressful and more effective. We become patient observers, waiting for the right moment to act, and when we do, we do so from a place of harmony and clarity. This is the true goal of harmonious trading: learning to trade in tune with the market, without forcing, without fighting, just flowing.

Inner Peace

Inner peace is one of the most important aspects for any trader who wants to be consistently successful. Although many people think that trading is just about numbers, charts, and strategies, in reality, the foundation of every good trader is in their mental and emotional state. Without inner peace, it is easy to get carried away by stress, anxiety, and the intense emotions that arise when we are in front of the market. Therefore, developing a calm and balanced mind is essential, not only to make better decisions, but also to maintain a healthy and sustainable relationship with trading over time.

When we talk about inner peace, we are not referring to the complete absence of problems or challenges. In trading, there will always be uncertainty, risks, and difficult moments. What we are looking for is to learn how to stay calm and centered in the midst of those challenges. Imagine a lake on a stormy day. On the surface, the water may be choppy, with waves and violent movements, but if we dive deeper, all is calm. The same is true of our mind. Although on the surface our emotions may be agitated by market volatility, deep down, we can find a place of calm and stability. And it is from that place that we want to trade.

Inner peace isn't something that just happens overnight. It's a state that is cultivated through daily practice. One of the most effective ways to achieve it is through meditation. Meditation teaches us to observe our thoughts and emotions without immediately reacting to them. In the context of trading, this is extremely valuable. When we're staring at the screen watching prices rise and fall, it's natural to feel a surge of emotions, from euphoria to fear. However, a trader who has cultivated inner peace through meditation is able to observe those feelings without getting swept up in them. Instead of making hasty or impulsive decisions, they can act from a place of calm and clarity.

But it's not just meditation that helps us develop inner peace. Self-care in general is also important. Many traders become so obsessed with the market that they forget to take care of their body and mind. They spend hours and hours in front of the screen, neglecting rest, nutrition, and physical exercise. This, over time, can lead to burnout and chronic stress, which negatively affects both trading performance and overall quality of life. That's why it's essential for traders to learn to disconnect from the market when necessary, to take a break, and to dedicate time to activities that relax and recharge their energy.

Another key to developing inner peace is learning to accept uncertainty. The market, by its nature, is unpredictable. No matter how much analysis we do, we can never be 100% sure of what is going to happen. This can lead to a great deal of stress, especially if we feel the need to control the outcome of every trade. However, a trader who has cultivated inner peace understands that uncertainty is part of the process and accepts it as such. He or she does not hold on to a fixed expectation about what should happen in the market. Instead of resisting uncertainty, he or she flows with it, knowing that if he or she stays calm and makes well-thought-out decisions, the long-term results will be positive.

Inner peace also has to do with how we handle our losses. In trading, losses are inevitable. No matter how good you are, there will always be trades that don't go as you expected. The difference between a successful trader and an unsuccessful one is often in the way they handle those losses. A trader without inner peace may fall into despair or panic when faced with a loss, and this leads them to make bad decisions in the future, impulsively trying to recover the lost money. On the other hand, a trader who has developed inner peace is able to accept loss with serenity. They don't see loss as a personal failure, but as part of learning and the natural cycle of the market.

Developing inner peace also helps us avoid the trap of greed. It is very easy, especially after a series of successful trades, to be tempted to risk more than necessary or to seek quick, big profits. However, greed often leads to unwise decisions that end in big losses. Inner peace keeps us focused on the process, rather than the immediate outcome. It helps us remember that trading is a long-distance race, not a sprint, and that the key to long-term success is patience and discipline, not the desire for quick profits.

A very useful tool for maintaining inner peace during trading sessions is conscious breathing. Throughout the day, and especially during high-intensity sessions, it is important to take a few minutes to breathe deeply and reconnect with the present. When we are nervous or stressed, our breathing becomes rapid and shallow, which only fuels our state of anxiety. By stopping and practicing deep, slow breathing, we can calm our nervous system, reduce stress, and return to a state of greater mental clarity. This can make a huge difference in how we approach our trading and how we react to market movements.

In short, inner peace is an essential component for any trader looking to succeed and enjoy the process. Not only does it help us make better decisions and avoid impulsive mistakes, but it also allows us to enjoy trading without being consumed by stress or frustration. Cultivating inner peace is a personal journey that takes time and dedication, but the benefits, both professionally and personally, are immense. When we operate from a place of calm and balance, we not only improve our results, but we also find a greater sense of satisfaction and well-being in everything we do.

Synchronization with Market Cycles

The market, like nature, has cycles. Just as we experience the seasons of the year in nature, with their own rhythms of growth and rest, the market also has times of expansion and contraction, of activity and stillness. Understanding these cycles is essential for any trader who wants to be consistently successful, but even more important is learning to synchronize ourselves with them. When we talk about "synchronizing with market cycles," we are talking about learning to trade in harmony with those rhythms, rather than trying to fight them.

Timing with market cycles means that instead of forcing our trades at any given moment, we wait for the right moments to act. It is not always the best time to enter a trade, just as it is not always the best time to sow in the wild. There are periods when the market is moving strongly, showing clear trends, and there are other times when it seems to be paused, with no apparent direction. Learning to recognize when the market is in a favorable cycle and when it is better to wait is one of the most important skills a trader can develop.

One of the most common mistakes traders make, especially those just starting out, is thinking that they should always be in the market. They believe that to be successful they must be constantly trading, looking for every little opportunity. However, this approach often leads to unnecessary mistakes and losses. The reality is that the market is not always offering good opportunities. Sometimes, the best decision we can make is to do nothing and wait for the cycle to change. Forcing a trade at a time when the market is in an unfavorable cycle is like planting seeds in winter, when the ground is frozen. No matter how much effort we put in, the results will not be as expected.

To synchronize ourselves with market cycles, the first thing we need to do is to observe carefully. Just as a farmer needs to observe the weather and the soil before planting, a trader must constantly observe the market before acting. This does not mean being glued to the screen all day, but rather learning to interpret the signals that the market gives us. Technical indicators, price trends and trading volume are some of the signals that can help us understand what cycle the market is in. However, in addition to these external signals, it is essential to develop an internal sensitivity, a kind of intuition that allows us to feel the rhythm of the market.

That intuition is not something mystical or magical. It is the result of experience and practice, of being constantly exposed to the market and observing how it behaves in different situations. Over time, we begin to notice patterns and cycles that repeat themselves. We start to realize when the market is in a bullish cycle, where prices tend to rise steadily, and when it is in a bearish cycle, where prices tend to fall. We can also identify consolidation cycles, where the market moves sideways, without a clear direction. These cycles are a natural part of the market, and learning to identify them is crucial to knowing when to act and when to wait.

Synchronizing ourselves with market cycles also means accepting that we have no control over them. Sometimes the market will show us clear opportunities and other times it will seem like everything is in chaos. It is in these moments of chaos and uncertainty that it is most important to remain calm and not give in to despair or fear. Just as we cannot control the seasons of the year, we cannot control market cycles either. Our job as traders is to observe, adapt and wait for the right moment to act.

One of the most well-known cycles in the market is the bull and bear cycle. During a bull cycle, prices rise steadily, driven by investor confidence and economic growth. This is a good time to look for buying opportunities, as the odds of making a profit are higher. However, it is important not to fall into the trap of thinking that the bull cycle will last forever. Every bull cycle eventually comes to an end, and when it does, it gives way to a bear cycle. During a bear cycle, prices fall, often quickly and aggressively. This is a time when many inexperienced traders lose money, because they fail to adjust to the change in cycle. However, traders who are in sync with the market know that bear cycles also offer opportunities, either to sell short or to wait until prices bottom out and start to rise again.

In addition to bull and bear cycles, there are other, more subtle cycles that we need to learn to identify. For example, high volatility and low volatility cycles. In a high volatility cycle, prices can move quickly in either direction, which can create great opportunities, but also great risks. At these times, it is important to be alert and prepared to react quickly. On the other hand, in a low volatility cycle, the market tends to move more slowly and predictably, which can be less exciting, but also safer for those who prefer a more conservative approach.

Timing with market cycles also requires patience. Many traders lose money simply because they do not have the patience to wait for the right cycle. They want to see immediate results, and in their quest for quick profits, they trade at times when the market is not offering good opportunities. Patience is a virtue in trading, and those who learn to wait for the right moment are the ones who achieve long-term success. Just as a fisherman knows that it is not always the best time to cast a line, a good trader knows that it is not always the right time to trade. Sometimes, the best course of action is to do nothing and wait for the market to show us the right cycle.

In short, timing with market cycles is an essential skill for any trader. It's not about predicting the future or controlling the market, but about learning to observe, adapt, and act at the right time. Market cycles are like waves in the ocean: we can't control them, but we can learn to ride them. If we synchronize with them, we can harness their power to our advantage. But if we try to fight them, we risk being swept away by the current. The key is to be in harmony with the market, flowing with its cycles, and making decisions from a place of calm and clarity.

Mindfulness in Real Time

Real-time mindfulness is one of the most powerful tools a trader can have at their disposal. While most people associate mindfulness with meditation or relaxation, its true strength lies in the ability to be fully present in the moment, without distractions, without judgment, and without being swept away by our emotions. In the world of trading, where decisions must be made in fractions of a second and where emotions can easily overwhelm us, this skill is essential to maintaining focus and mental clarity.

The concept of real-time mindfulness refers to the practice of being completely aware of what is happening while trading in the market. This means being aware of every move, every decision, and every emotion that arises within us. Instead of letting our minds get distracted by thoughts about the past or the future, mindfulness helps us stay focused on what is happening right now. This is crucial because, in trading, the only thing that really matters is the present moment. The market is constantly changing, and if our mind is caught up in what happened a few minutes ago or worried about what might happen next, we miss the opportunity to act effectively.

One of the main benefits of real-time mindfulness is that it helps us reduce the influence of our emotions on our decisions. Trading is an emotionally intense activity. Prices go up, prices go down, and in a matter of seconds we can go from feeling euphoria to fear. These emotions are natural, but if we let them control us, we can make impulsive and often wrong decisions. For example, fear of losing money can lead us to close a trade too soon, while greed can push us to hold a position for longer than necessary. Mindfulness allows us to observe these emotions without immediately reacting to them. By being aware of what we are feeling, we can take a moment to breathe, assess the situation objectively, and then act from a place of calm and control.

Practicing mindfulness in real time starts with something as simple as breathing. Throughout the day, and especially during a trading session, it's easy for our breathing to become shallow and rapid due to stress. This, in turn, fuels anxiety and mental confusion. But when we practice mindfulness, we make a conscious effort to maintain deep, controlled breathing. Whenever we notice our mind starting to race or our emotions starting to run high, we can return our attention to our breathing. By consciously inhaling and exhaling, we not only calm our body, but we also clear our mind, allowing us to come back to the present and make better decisions.

Another key aspect of real-time mindfulness is the ability to observe our thoughts without identifying with them. In trading, our mind is constantly generating thoughts: "Should I enter this trade?", "What if I lose money?", "Maybe I should have waited a little longer." These thoughts can be overwhelming if we don't learn to manage them. Mindfulness teaches us to see those thoughts as simple mental events, not absolute truths. We don't have to act on every thought that comes up. By observing them from a mental distance, we can decide which ones are useful and which ones aren't. This allows us to act more logically and less impulsively.

Real-time mindfulness also helps us stay focused on the process, rather than obsessing over the results. One of the biggest mistakes traders make is focusing too much on immediate gains or losses. If we are constantly worried about how much money we are making or losing on each trade, we lose sight of the bigger picture and often make poor decisions. Mindfulness invites us to shift our attention to the process of making good decisions. By being present at every step, from initial analysis to trade execution, we ensure that we are trading in a disciplined and strategic manner, without being distracted by the end result.

The key to real-time mindfulness is consistent practice. It's not something you learn overnight, and it's not something you can just do once in a while. Like any other skill, mindfulness takes time and dedication to develop. An easy way to get started is to incorporate short mindfulness breaks throughout your trading day. These breaks don't have to be long—even a few minutes of conscious breathing or just being present without doing anything can make a huge difference in how you handle stress and make decisions.

Imagine that the market is in a phase of high volatility, and you feel like your emotions are starting to get the best of you. At that moment, instead of rushing into a decision based on fear or greed, you could stop for a moment, take a few deep breaths, and ask yourself, "Am I operating from a place of clarity or from a place of anxiety?" This small space of time, this conscious pause, can be the difference between an impulsive decision and a well-thought-out decision.

Another way to practice mindfulness in real time is to pay attention to our body's physical cues. Often, our body gives us clues about our emotional state before we consciously notice it. For example, you might notice that your muscles are tense, that you're clenching your teeth, or that your heart is beating rapidly. These are signs that you're under stress and might be about to make an emotional decision. By noticing these cues, you can stop, relax, and return to the present moment before you act.

In short, real-time mindfulness is an invaluable tool for any trader looking to trade more effectively and less emotionally. It helps us to be present in the moment, to observe our emotions without getting carried away by them, and to make decisions from a place of calm and clarity. It's not about eliminating emotions or thoughts, but rather learning to manage them in a way that doesn't interfere with our performance. With consistent practice, mindfulness allows us to trade with more focus, less stress, and ultimately, greater success in the market. When we are truly present in the now, we are able to see the market as it is, without the distortions of our emotions or thoughts, and this allows us to trade with a precision and clarity that would otherwise be impossible.

The Harmony between Risk and Reward

The balance between risk and reward is one of the most important principles that a trader must understand and apply in their daily life. In trading, every trade we make involves risk, and with that risk comes the possibility of reward. Finding the balance between the two is critical to long-term success. It is very easy to fall into the trap of focusing only on the potential gains and forgetting about the risks we are taking. However, a wise trader knows that in order to prosper, they must manage risk carefully, making sure it is in proportion to the expected reward.

When we talk about risk and reward, we are referring to the relationship between how much we are willing to lose on a trade and how much we expect to gain. This relationship is the foundation of any successful trading strategy. While it may seem appealing to aim for big rewards, we need to be realistic and understand that the bigger the potential gain, the bigger the risk. It is not about avoiding risk altogether, as risk is an inherent part of trading. It is about managing that risk intelligently and making sure that the potential rewards justify the decisions we are making.

For many new traders, the initial focus is often on maximizing profits at any cost. They get excited about the idea of making big profits quickly and often end up risking too much on a single trade. This may work in the short term, but over time, it often leads to big losses. A trader who risks too much without calculating the risk can lose everything on a single trade, no matter how many times they have won before. The key is to find a balance point, a harmony between how much we are willing to risk and how much we can win on each trade.

The first step to achieving this harmony is to establish a clear plan for each trade. This means deciding in advance what our maximum risk will be and what reward we are looking for. Many experienced traders use a risk-reward ratio of at least 1:2 or 1:3. This means that for every dollar they are willing to lose, they expect to win at least two or three. This way, even if they lose more trades than they win, they will still be profitable in the long run, as the rewards will outweigh the losses.

It's important to remember that not every trade is going to be a winner, and that's okay. Part of the art of trading is accepting that some trades are going to result in losses. The goal isn't to win on every trade, but to make sure that when we do win, the profits are large enough to cover the losses. If we maintain a healthy risk-reward ratio, we can afford to lose on some trades and still end up with a profit at the end of the day or week.

To achieve harmony between risk and reward, it is also essential to know our own limits and risk tolerance. Not all traders have the same ability to manage risk. Some are comfortable taking on more risk in the hope of greater rewards, while others prefer a more conservative approach, with lower risks and more modest rewards. Neither of these approaches is necessarily better than the other; the important thing is that it is consistent with our personality and trading style. If we are constantly nervous or worried about the risk we are taking, we are probably not trading effectively. Trading should be a process in which we feel in control and comfortable with the decisions we are making.

A common mistake that many traders make is adjusting their risk once they are already in a trade. For example, they start with a clear idea of how much they are willing to risk, but when the market moves against them, they decide to increase their stop loss, hoping that the trade will eventually turn around. This is dangerous, as it goes against the principle of risk-reward harmony. If we arbitrarily increase our risk, we break the balance and expose ourselves to larger losses than we were initially prepared to take. It is essential to set our risk limits before entering a trade and to stick to them, no matter what.

Discipline plays a crucial role in maintaining the harmony between risk and reward. It is not enough to have a plan; we must be able to follow that plan even when the market tests us. Sometimes, the market will make us doubt our decisions, and it is at such times that discipline and confidence in our strategy become essential. If we have done our analysis and have established a reasonable risk-reward ratio, we must trust our process and not get carried away by the emotions of the moment.

Another important aspect to keep in mind is that not all trades require the same level of risk. In some cases, we may see an opportunity that has a high potential for reward with relatively low risk. In other situations, we might be willing to take on a higher risk if we believe the reward opportunity justifies it. The important thing is to be flexible and adjust our risk based on the situation, always maintaining the balance between risk and reward.

It is also essential to learn how to diversify our trades. Putting all of our capital into a single trade is extremely risky. Even if the trade seems like a safe bet, the market can surprise us at any moment. By diversifying our trades and not risking too much in any one trade, we can protect ourselves from catastrophic losses and maintain a constant flow of opportunities. Diversification allows us to spread risk more evenly, which helps us maintain the balance between risk and reward.

Finally, to maintain a good balance between risk and reward, it is important to keep an eye on how the market changes. The market is not static; it is constantly evolving, and what worked yesterday may not work today. That is why it is essential to be willing to adjust our risk and reward strategies as the market changes. This does not mean changing our rules on every trade, but rather being open to reviewing our strategies over the long term to ensure that they remain effective in the current environment.

In short, the harmony between risk and reward is essential for any trader looking to be consistently successful. It's not just about chasing big profits, but about managing risk in a balanced and responsible way. When we manage to find that balance, we can trade with more confidence, knowing that our losses will be controlled and that our rewards, when they come, will be large enough to justify the risk taken. Maintaining this harmony is not easy, but with discipline, planning, and patience, we can ensure that our trades are always aligned with our long-term goals.

The Trader's Sixth Sense

The trader's sixth sense is something that many have heard of, but few fully understand. Over the years, many experienced traders have described moments when they simply "knew" they should act, even when there was no apparent logical or technical reason to do so. This sixth sense is not a magical ability or supernatural power; it is a kind of intuition developed through experience and constant practice. As a trader becomes more familiar with the market, he or she begins to pick up on subtle patterns and signals that are not always visible to the naked eye. This sense, while difficult to explain, can become a valuable tool if you know how to listen to it and use it properly.

Over time, a trader can develop a deeper connection with the market, to the point where decisions begin to flow naturally. This feeling of "knowing what to do" for no apparent reason comes from the accumulation of knowledge and constant observation. When a trader spends hours, days, and years observing charts, price movements, and market reactions, his or her brain begins to identify patterns that are not always apparent on a conscious level. These patterns are stored in the subconscious, and when they occur again, the trader experiences that feeling that something is about to happen, even if he or she cannot always explain it in words.

A trader's sixth sense doesn't just come out of nowhere; it requires a solid foundation of technical knowledge and experience. A novice trader who hasn't spent enough time in the market can mistake his emotions or desires for intuition, often leading to impulsive and ill-informed decisions. True sixth sense develops as a trader gains a deeper understanding of the markets and himself. This intuition is based on knowledge, not chance. It's the result of having seen enough similar situations and learned from them, of having failed, adjusted, and improved.

One of the main challenges traders face when they begin to develop this sixth sense is differentiating between real intuition and emotions that can cloud their judgment. Fear, greed, and anxiety are common emotions in trading, and if left unchecked, they can lead us to make decisions based on impulse rather than logic or intuition. For the sixth sense to work effectively, it is crucial for the trader to have a clear mind free from emotional influences. Only when we have learned to manage our emotions and trade from a place of calm and focus, can we trust our intuition to guide us at the right time.

A key aspect of a trader's sixth sense is learning to trust it. Many times, a trader may have that inner feeling that something is about to change in the market, but hesitate to act because they can't find a logical or technical reason to back it up. In these cases, the trader may feel torn between their rational knowledge and their intuition. However, over time, those who develop a strong sixth sense learn to trust their instinct, especially when they feel it is based on prior experience. This doesn't mean ignoring technical or fundamental analysis, but rather using intuition as an additional tool that complements the others.

It's important to note that your sixth sense isn't infallible. Even the most experienced traders who rely on their intuition will make mistakes from time to time. The market is unpredictable, and while intuition can help us make better decisions, it doesn't guarantee success on every trade. What it does do is give us an extra edge, a way of perceiving the market that goes beyond what's on display. On many occasions, that little internal signal can be the difference between a successful trade and a losing one.

Another crucial factor in developing the sixth sense is patience. It is not something that develops overnight, nor is it something that can be forced. It is a process that takes time and requires dedication. A trader who wants to develop this intuition must be willing to learn from each trade, both the wins and the losses. Every experience, every mistake, and every success contributes to that inner knowledge that eventually becomes intuition. Therefore, it is essential for the trader to adopt a constant learning mindset and not be discouraged by losses or mistakes. Each of those moments is an opportunity to hone that sixth sense.

The environment in which we operate can also influence the development of the sixth sense. A quiet, distraction-free workspace helps a trader concentrate better and be more in tune with the market. In addition, maintaining a disciplined and well-structured trading routine facilitates the process of identifying patterns and developing sharper intuition. Clutter, lack of concentration, or constant stress can block this ability to perceive the market more deeply. This is why many successful traders also practice relaxation, meditation, or mindfulness techniques, as these practices help clear the mind and be more present in the moment.

One of the keys to making the most of your sixth sense is knowing when to act and when to wait. Not every gut feeling needs to be followed immediately. Sometimes that gut feeling can be a warning for us to pay more attention, but not necessarily for us to act right away. A good trader knows when his gut is telling him it's time to make a decision and when he should simply watch and wait a little longer. Developing this ability to discern is essential to avoid impulsive mistakes and to maximize the profit from trading.

Finally, it is important to remember that a trader's sixth sense is a skill that can be improved over time, but is never completely "finished." The market is constantly changing, and a trader who is not willing to continue learning and adapting will lose his connection with it. That is why intuition should be seen as a dynamic tool that adjusts and evolves with experience. As the market changes, we must also adjust the way we perceive it and react to its movements.

In short, a trader's sixth sense is a combination of experience, observation, and deep connection with the market. It is not something that can be taught in a book or a course, but it can be developed over time through practice and continuous learning. This sense, when properly cultivated, can become a powerful tool for navigating market challenges and making better decisions. While not infallible, the sixth sense can provide a significant advantage in an environment as dynamic and competitive as trading, helping a trader anticipate moves, better manage risk, and ultimately find more success in their trading.

55

Creative Visualization

Creative visualization is a powerful tool that many traders have begun to incorporate into their daily routine to improve their performance and connection with the market. Essentially, it involves clearly and in detail imagining the results you want to achieve, seeing in your mind how successful trades unfold before they happen. This practice is based on the idea that our mind has a direct impact on our actions. If we are able to visualize success, our decisions and behaviors in the market will begin to align with that mental image we have created. But creative visualization is not just imagining everything going perfectly; it is a way to mentally prepare ourselves for different scenarios, train our mind, and increase our confidence when trading.

To begin practicing creative visualization, the first thing you need to do is find a quiet space where you can relax and focus. It is important to be in a calm state of mind that is free from distractions. Many traders choose to do this practice at the start of the day or just before starting a trading session, so that they are mentally prepared and focused. Creative visualization does not require much time; even a few minutes can be enough to have a positive impact on your mental state.

Once you are in a relaxed state, the next step is to start visualizing the type of trades you want to make. Imagine that you are sitting in front of your screen, looking at charts and analyzing the market. Visualize how you read the data clearly, how you identify the right signals and make decisions based on your analysis. It is important that this visualization is as detailed as possible. Imagine the environment around you, the colors of the charts, the sound of the keyboard, even how you physically feel while making each trade. The more details you can add, the more effective the visualization will be.

A key aspect of creative visualization is imagining not only the moments of success, but also the challenges you might face. For example, you might visualize how you react to a trade that doesn't go as planned. Instead of panicking, you see yourself staying calm, assessing the situation logically, and making smart decisions to mitigate risk. This type of visualization not only prepares you for successes, but also for difficult moments, helping you develop a more balanced and resilient mindset.

Another important element of creative visualization is imagining how you feel emotionally throughout the trading process. Often, the biggest obstacle we face as traders is not the market itself, but our own emotions. Feeling afraid, anxious or stressed can cloud our judgment and lead us to make mistakes. That is why, during visualization, it is essential that you imagine yourself trading with complete confidence and serenity. You can visualize how you breathe deeply before each trade, how you stay calm even when the market is volatile and how you act in a firm and decisive manner, without being carried away by emotions.

Repetition is key for creative visualization to have a lasting impact. Just like any skill, the more you practice it, the more effective it becomes. If you visualize consistently, your mind will begin to adopt these behavioral patterns as part of your regular routine. At first, it may not seem like it is having an immediate effect, but over time you will begin to notice how your confidence increases and how you feel more prepared to face the challenges of the market. This does not mean that all of your trades will be perfect, but you will be more mentally and emotionally prepared to handle them.

In addition to visualizing individual trades, you can also use this technique to visualize your long-term goals as a trader. For example, if your goal is to reach a certain level of profitability or consistency in your trading, you can imagine yourself achieving that goal. Visualize how you feel about reaching that goal, what changes you've made to your trading routine, and how you've improved over time. This type of visualization helps keep you focused on your goals and reminds you that success doesn't come overnight, but rather as a result of a continuous process of learning and improvement.

Creative visualization can also help you overcome moments of doubt or uncertainty. All traders go through phases when things don't go as expected, and it can be easy to get discouraged or lose confidence. At these times, visualizing your past success or future potential can be an effective way to regain motivation and clarity. By remembering times when you've traded successfully and imagining future achievements, you can reprogram your mind to focus on the positive rather than the difficulties.

It is important to note that creative visualization is not a substitute for hard work, analysis, or discipline. It is not a magic solution to trading success. However, when combined with a solid strategy, good analysis, and strict discipline, it can become a very powerful tool. Creative visualization helps you improve your mindset, be more present in the moment, and make decisions with greater clarity and confidence.

It's also helpful to remember that creative visualization isn't exclusive to trading. Many athletes, entrepreneurs, and people in various professions use this technique to improve their performance. What makes it work in trading is the way it helps you manage the stress and pressure of quick decisions, as well as maintaining a positive, focused attitude over the long term.

Finally, creative visualization is a skill that can evolve over time. At first, you may find it difficult to imagine certain details or maintain concentration. This is completely normal. As you continue to practice, you will become more skilled at visualization and will be able to do it with greater ease and clarity. The important thing is to be consistent and make it part of your daily trading routine.

In conclusion, creative visualization is a simple yet extremely powerful technique that can help you improve your performance as a trader. By taking the time to imagine your trades in a detailed and positive way, you are training your mind to be more prepared, confident, and focused on success. While it does not guarantee immediate results, with time and practice, you will notice a difference in how you approach the market, how you manage your emotions, and how you make decisions. Much like technical analysis or risk management, creative visualization is another tool you can add to your arsenal to become a more well-rounded and successful trader.

Emotional Management

Emotional management is one of the most crucial aspects of trading, yet it is often overlooked. In any trade, whether it is a successful day or a challenging one, our emotions play an immense role in the decisions we make. Sometimes, the difference between a successful trade and one that results in a loss is not technical analysis or strategy, but how we manage our emotions at key moments. However, the good news is that, like other skills, emotional management can be learned and honed over time.

The first thing we need to recognize is that trading is an emotionally charged activity. Every time we open a trade, we are facing uncertainty and risk. No matter how well prepared you are or how much experience you have, the market always has a level of unpredictability that can generate anxiety, fear, excitement or even euphoria. These emotions are natural and should not be ignored. Pretending that we do not feel anything while trading would be counterproductive. The secret is not to suppress emotions, but to learn to manage them constructively.

One of the most common emotions in trading is fear. Fear can manifest itself in many ways: fear of losing money, fear of making a mistake, or fear of not meeting our expectations. Fear can be paralyzing, causing us to doubt our decisions or stray from our strategy. To manage fear, it is important to develop a healthy relationship with it. We cannot eliminate fear completely, but we can learn to recognize it and act despite it. One of the best ways to do this is to trust our trading plan and prior preparation. When we have a clear strategy and have practiced discipline, fear loses some of its power because we know that our decisions are based on solid analysis and not emotional impulses.

On the other hand, there is also the opposite problem: euphoria. When trades are going well and everything seems to be lining up in our favor, it is easy to fall into a feeling of invincibility. The problem with euphoria is that it can lead us to take unnecessary risks or to stray from our strategy. Feeling good about our wins is natural, but it is important to remember that success in trading is not measured by a single trade, but by consistency over time. Euphoria can cloud our judgment and make us forget that the market can change at any moment. The key here is to stay grounded and remember that each trade is independent and should be treated with the same level of attention and care.

A very dangerous emotion in trading is frustration. We've all had days when, no matter what we do, it seems like everything is going against us. Maybe the market doesn't behave the way we expected, or maybe we make consecutive mistakes that affect our performance. At these times, frustration can build up and cause us to react impulsively. This is where many traders fall into the mistake of "getting revenge" on the market, trying to quickly recoup losses with trades that are not well thought out. This attitude can be disastrous and lead us to lose even more money. The best way to handle frustration is to recognize when we need a break. Sometimes, stepping away from the market for a while and clearing our mind is the wisest decision we can make. We'll come back with a clearer and less emotional mindset.

Greed is another emotion that can affect our decision-making. In trading, greed manifests itself when we struggle to close a winning trade because we want to squeeze out every last cent of profit, or when we take on more risk than necessary in the hopes of making big profits quickly. This mindset can lead us to miss opportunities to secure profits or, worse, lose money because the market takes an unexpected turn. To combat greed, it is essential to have a clear exit strategy and stick to it. Knowing when enough is enough and being satisfied with a reasonable profit is a skill every trader must develop to stay in the game for the long term.

Another essential part of emotional management is learning to accept losses. In trading, losses are inevitable. No matter how well we do our analysis or how careful our strategy is, there will be times when things don't go our way. The difference between a successful trader and an unsuccessful one often lies in how they handle those losses. Instead of seeing a loss as a personal failure or a sign that we're not good enough, we should see it as part of the learning process. Every loss is an opportunity to evaluate what went wrong, adjust our strategy if necessary, and move on without carrying the emotional baggage of that outcome. It's important to remember that one losing trade doesn't define our worth as traders.

Patience is one of the most important virtues a trader can have when it comes to emotional management. The market will not always move according to our timing or expectations, and there will be times when no clear opportunity presents itself. In these cases, impatience can lead us to force trades in markets that do not have good odds in our favor. Patience allows us to wait for the right moment to act, trusting that opportunities will come when the time is right. Developing this patience takes practice and self-control, but in the long run it will save us a lot of frustration and unnecessary losses.

One of the best ways to improve our emotional management is through self-observation. Just as we analyze the market, we should analyze our own emotions and behavioral patterns. What do we feel before, during, and after each trade? Which emotions tend to influence our decisions the most? By asking ourselves these questions, we can begin to identify emotional patterns that negatively affect us. For example, we might find that we tend to be too conservative after a loss or too aggressive after a win. By being aware of these patterns, we can begin to work on them and develop greater self-awareness.

It's also helpful to have a daily routine that helps us manage our emotions. This can include practices like meditation, exercise, or simply taking a few minutes before each trading session to breathe deeply and calm the mind. These practices help us get into a more balanced state of mind, allowing us to make clearer, more rational decisions. It's not necessary to spend a lot of time on these activities, but doing them consistently can make a big difference in how we feel and how we react in the market.

Finally, it is crucial to remember that emotional management is an ongoing process. We will never reach a point where we can say that we have completely mastered our emotions. The market will always present new challenges and unexpected situations that will test our ability to remain calm and clear. The important thing is to be committed to constant improvement and be willing to learn from every experience, whether positive or negative. At the end of the day, our emotions are part of what makes us human, and learning to manage them in the context of trading is what will allow us to achieve long-term success.

In short, emotional management in trading is essential to keep us focused, disciplined, and prepared for the ups and downs we will inevitably encounter. By learning to recognize and manage our emotions constructively, we not only improve our performance in the market, but we also become more balanced and conscious traders. The key is constant practice, self-awareness, and the willingness to adapt and learn at every stage of the way.

Waiting for the Right Moment

Waiting for the right moment is one of the most valuable lessons any trader can learn, but also one of the most difficult to put into practice. The market is constantly moving, filled with opportunities that appear and disappear in a matter of seconds. For many, this speed can be overwhelming and lead to the feeling that we are always missing out on something important. However, the reality is that not all opportunities are good, and knowing when to act and when to wait can make the difference between a successful trade and a costly loss.

One of the most common mistakes traders, especially beginners, tend to make is entering the market on impulse. Sometimes it's the fear of missing out (what many call "FOMO," or fear of missing out) that leads us to make hasty trades. Other times, it's the anxiety of wanting to do something, anything, instead of sitting still. But trading isn't a race of speed, it's a race of patience. The ability to wait for the right moment not only saves you from wrong trades, but allows you to make decisions based on solid analysis and strategy instead of emotions or pressure of the moment.

Waiting for the right time means understanding that not every day or time is optimal for trading. The market has cycles, patterns, and behaviors that change throughout the day and week. For example, you might specialize in trading during certain times of the day, such as the opening of the markets in New York or London, where volatility is higher and opportunities are clearer. Or you might prefer to trade in calmer markets, where movements are more predictable. Whatever your approach, the important thing to understand is that there won't always be an opportunity that fits your strategy, and it's okay to wait until the conditions are right.

The problem with acting without waiting for the right moment is that we often rely on a need to be busy or to feel like we are making progress. But in trading, less is often more. Impulsive trades based on impatience tend to lead to losses or suboptimal results. An experienced trader knows that being in front of the screen does not necessarily mean trading all the time. In fact, a large part of effective trading is about observing, analyzing, and waiting. The key is to develop the ability to recognize when the market is not presenting favorable conditions and having the discipline to refrain from acting.

An important aspect of waiting for the right moment is learning to identify patterns and signals that tell you when is the best time to enter or exit a trade. Many traders use technical analysis to look for these ideal moments. However, even with solid analysis, the best opportunities will not always appear immediately. You may spend hours or even days waiting for a perfect setup to materialize. During this time, it is critical not to be tempted to rush or force a trade just out of a desire to be active in the market. Patience is key here.

It's also important to recognize that the market won't always be aligned with your expectations. Sometimes, it may seem like all the indicators are in place and a trade is imminent, only for the market to do something completely unexpected. These are the times when patience is tested. Instead of trying to guess or get ahead of moves, it's best to wait for the market to give you clear confirmation. Often, waiting for an additional signal or one more small move can prevent you from falling into a trap or getting caught in a trend that isn't sustainable.

Another advantage of waiting for the right time is that it helps you manage risk more effectively. When you act patiently and only enter the market when conditions are optimal, you reduce the chance of making impulsive mistakes. You know that every trade you make is backed by careful analysis and that you have chosen the best possible time to enter. This does not guarantee that all your trades will be winners, but it significantly increases the odds of success and allows you to have more precise control over your decisions.

Waiting for the right time doesn't just apply to entering the market, but also to exiting it. Knowing when to close a trade is just as important as knowing when to open one. Sometimes, it's easy to get carried away by the excitement when a trade is going well and continue holding it in search of more profits. However, this can lead to losing out on accumulated profits when the market takes an unexpected turn. So, part of waiting for the right time is knowing when enough is enough and when it's time to take your profits or accept a small loss before it turns into something bigger.

The patience you develop by waiting for the right moment also has a positive effect on your mental state. Instead of constantly worrying or stressing about every market move, you give yourself permission to relax and observe. You know that you don't have to take advantage of every little opportunity that comes along and that it's okay to wait for the ones that are actually worthwhile. This calmer approach not only improves your decision-making, but it also reduces burnout and stress in the long run, allowing you to stay focused and in control.

It's also important to mention that waiting for the right moment doesn't mean being completely inactive. During this time, you can be honing your skills, adjusting your strategy, reviewing your past trades, or even learning more about the markets. This waiting time is an opportunity to better prepare yourself, to fine-tune your approach, and to make sure that you're ready when the right opportunity finally presents itself. It's a mindset of continuous preparation, not passivity.

Some traders even view the act of waiting as part of the trading process itself. Instead of feeling like they are wasting their time while waiting, they view this time as an investment in their long-term success. Waiting for the right moment is an active decision, a crucial part of their strategy that allows them to maximize their opportunities and minimize their mistakes. This perspective completely changes the way we view downtime in the market, and helps us become more disciplined and strategic in our actions.

Lastly, the patience required to wait for the right moment also extends to how we approach our growth as traders. Success in trading doesn't come overnight, and trying to rush the process only leads to frustration and mistakes. Just like in the market, in our trading careers, we must also learn to wait for the right moment. Every trade, every lesson, every mistake is part of a larger journey that requires time, effort, and most of all, patience.

In short, waiting for the right moment is an essential skill for any trader who wants to achieve long-term success. It involves having the discipline to observe the market calmly, make decisions based on analysis rather than emotions, and know when to act and when to refrain. By mastering this skill, we not only improve our performance in the market, but we also develop a more balanced, patient, and strategic mindset. And it is this mindset that will ultimately lead us to achieve our goals as traders.

Connection with Purpose

Connecting with purpose is one of the fundamental pillars to be successful in trading and, in general, in any aspect of life. When we talk about purpose in the context of trading, we are not just referring to the desire to make money or generate income. Purpose is much deeper. It is that internal motivation that goes beyond immediate results and that drives us to keep going, even when things don't go as we expect. Having a clear purpose gives us direction, allows us to stay focused and, most importantly, helps us navigate difficulties with greater mental and emotional strength.

When you're starting out in trading, it's easy to fall into the trap of focusing solely on the technical aspects: the charts, the indicators, the trends. But over time, many traders realize that mastering these elements isn't enough. You need something more, a connection to a deeper purpose that guides your decisions and sustains your long-term motivation. Trading the markets can be exhausting and challenging, and it's in those moments of difficulty that purpose becomes your anchor.

Purpose in trading is not just about achieving financial goals, but also about understanding why we want to be traders in the first place. What drives us to participate in this dynamic and sometimes unpredictable world? For some, it may be financial freedom, the ability to work from anywhere and not be dependent on a traditional job. For others, it may be the intellectual challenge it represents, the constant learning and adaptation it requires. Whatever the reason, connecting with that purpose gives us a clear reason to keep going, even on the toughest days.

It is important to realize that purpose is not something we find overnight. It is something that develops over time, as we grow as traders and as people. At first, many enter trading with the simple idea of making money quickly, but they soon discover that there is much more at stake. Trading is a journey of self-discovery. We confront not only the market, but also ourselves, our emotions, our fears, and our limitations. It is in this process that we begin to connect with a more authentic and personal purpose.

Having a clear purpose also helps us maintain discipline. Trading requires a high level of self-control and focus. There are times when things don't go as planned, and it's easy to lose motivation or stray from our strategy. However, when we have a strong purpose, we remind ourselves why we're doing what we're doing. It allows us to stay focused and disciplined, even when the market is volatile or when we experience a losing streak. Instead of giving up, we lean on that purpose to keep learning and improving.

Another important aspect of purpose connection is that it helps us make decisions that are more aligned with our values. Often in trading, we can be tempted to take shortcuts or take unnecessary risks in pursuit of a quick profit. But if we are connected to our purpose, our decisions tend to be more thoughtful and careful. We don't act impulsively or get carried away by fear or greed. Instead, our actions are aligned with a larger, and ultimately more sustainable, goal.

Connecting with purpose also helps us find meaning in our experiences, even the most difficult ones. In trading, there will be losses, failures, and moments of frustration. If we focus only on immediate results, these challenges can be daunting and difficult to overcome. But when we trade with purpose, we understand that every experience, good or bad, is part of a larger process. Losses become lessons, frustrations become opportunities to grow and improve. Purpose gives us a long-term perspective, allowing us to view trading as a long-distance race rather than a series of short-term results.

The process of connecting with our purpose also invites us to reflect on what kind of traders we want to be. Do we want to be traders who are only looking to make quick profits, no matter the cost? Or do we want to be traders who operate with integrity, who are committed to learning, growing, and developing sustainable skills over time? These are important questions to ask ourselves as we move forward on our path. Our purpose will help us make decisions that are aligned with who we are and the vision we have for our future in the market.

Furthermore, purpose gives us a sense of inner peace. When we are connected to a clear purpose, we don't need to compare ourselves to other traders or worry about the success of others. We know that we are on our own path, following our own pace. Success in trading is not measured solely by the money we make, but also by how we feel in the process. A strong purpose allows us to enjoy the journey more, learn to appreciate both the victories and the challenges, and stay focused on what really matters.

It's essential to remember that our purpose can evolve over time. What motivates us today may not be the same thing that motivates us in a few years. As we gain more trading experience and wisdom, our goals and vision may change. And that's okay. The key is to always stay in tune with ourselves and our motivations. Taking the time to regularly reflect on why we do what we do allows us to adjust our approach and maintain a constant connection to our purpose.

For some traders, purpose may go beyond trading itself. Perhaps trading is a tool that allows them to achieve other goals in life, such as having more time to spend with family, traveling, or pursuing other passions. In this sense, trading is not the end, but rather the means to a more fulfilling and satisfying life. When we look at trading from this broader perspective, we realize that it's not all about the trades we make or the numbers in our account. It's about how trading aligns with our life and the overall purpose we have.

In conclusion, connecting with our purpose is one of the most important elements to success and satisfaction in trading. It gives us clarity, discipline, peace of mind, and a long-term perspective that helps us deal with both market ups and downs and personal challenges. Beyond financial gains, trading with a purpose allows us to find meaning and satisfaction in every step of the way, making the journey worthwhile in itself. And, most importantly, it gives us a reason to keep going, even when the road gets tough, because we know we are chasing something bigger than ourselves.

The Philosophy of Detachment

The philosophy of detachment is one of the most powerful and transformative concepts a trader can learn. At first glance, it may seem counterintuitive, as in trading we are constantly making decisions that involve money, risk, and emotions. However, detachment does not mean that we do not care about what we do or that we are indifferent to the outcome. Rather, detachment means learning not to be emotionally attached to our trades, whether they are profits or losses, and developing a mindset where the process and discipline matter more than individual outcomes. It is a state of serenity and equanimity that allows us to make better decisions and avoid unnecessary stress.

In the world of trading, it's easy to fall into the trap of becoming emotionally attached to our trades. When a trade goes well, we feel euphoria; when it goes badly, we feel frustration or even despair. This emotional roller coaster is not only exhausting, it also clouds our judgment. A trader who is too attached to the results of their trades runs the risk of making decisions based on their emotions rather than based on objective analysis and a clear strategy. This is where detachment comes in – learning to accept the outcome, whatever it may be, and move on without letting emotions cloud your judgment.

Being detached in trading doesn't mean we don't care about our trades or aren't committed to the process. What it means is that we aren't fixated on the immediate outcome. Instead of measuring our success or failure based on an individual trade, we look at the bigger picture. We know that trading is a game of probability, and there will be winning and losing trades. It's not about each individual trade that's important, but about the consistency and discipline with which we apply our strategy over time.

One of the ways that detachment benefits us is by helping us avoid emotional bias. When we are too attached to a trade, we can fall into the trap of holding it open longer than necessary, hoping that the market will move in our favor. Or we may close a winning trade too soon for fear of losing what we have already gained. These impulsive decisions, based on emotional attachment, often lead to suboptimal outcomes. By detaching ourselves, we are able to make more objective decisions, based on the facts and our analysis, rather than being driven by fear or greed.

Detachment also allows us to accept losses in a healthier way. Losses are an inevitable part of trading, and no trader, no matter how experienced, is immune to them. However, when we are too attached to our trades, a loss can feel like a personal blow, something that affects us deeply. This can lead to frustration, stress, and self-doubt about our abilities. But when we adopt the philosophy of detachment, we understand that a loss does not define our worth as traders or as people. It is simply a part of the process. The key is to learn from those losses, adjust our strategies if necessary, and move forward without getting stuck in the past.

An important aspect of detachment is also learning to let go of control. In trading, there are many factors that are outside of our control: market movements, economic news, global events, and so on. Trying to control every aspect of what happens in the market is a futile and frustrating task. By detaching, we accept that we cannot control the market, but we can control how we react to it. We focus on what is within our control, such as our strategy, our emotions, and our discipline. By letting go of the need to control everything, we free ourselves from a lot of unnecessary stress and pressure.

Another way that detachment helps us is by keeping a long-term mindset. Trading is not a sprint, it's a marathon. When we're too attached to short-term results, we can lose sight of the bigger picture. Maybe a trade doesn't go the way we expected, but that doesn't mean our strategy is wrong or that we're on the wrong path. By detaching, we allow ourselves to be patient and trust the long-term process. We know there will be ups and downs, but the important thing is to maintain consistency and discipline over time.

Detaching also helps us maintain greater peace of mind. Trading can be stressful and demanding, but when we detach ourselves from the immediate results, we reduce the level of stress we feel. Instead of living each trade as if it were a life-or-death event, we see it simply as a part of the overall process. This allows us to remain calm, even in the most volatile times of the market. And when we are calmer, we are able to make clearer, more rational decisions.

One of the biggest challenges in becoming detached is that it requires mental reprogramming. Throughout our lives, we have been conditioned to measure success based on tangible, immediate results. We want to see profits, we want to feel validated by our decisions. But in trading, this mindset can backfire. True success in trading is not measured by a winning trade, but by our ability to stay consistent, disciplined, and focused over the long term. Detaching ourselves from immediate results allows us to operate from a place of greater clarity and internal control.

A common example of emotional attachment is when a trade starts to go against us. Instead of accepting the small loss and getting out, some traders cling to the hope that the market will turn around. This emotional attachment to the trade can lead to much larger losses than we had originally planned. Detachment, on the other hand, allows us to cut losses quickly and without emotion, because we understand that a small loss is not the end of the world, it is simply part of the game.

Furthermore, detachment allows us to enjoy the process more. When we are too focused on the results, every trade becomes a source of anxiety. But when we detach ourselves from the results, we can begin to enjoy the intellectual and emotional challenge that trading represents. We see each trade as an opportunity to learn, grow, and improve our skills. The process becomes more than just making or losing money; it becomes a journey of self-discovery and personal growth.

Ultimately, the philosophy of detachment not only improves our trading performance, but also our quality of life. When we are too attached to market outcomes, we carry that stress and anxiety into other areas of our lives. But by detaching, we not only free ourselves in the realm of trading, but we also bring that peace of mind and serenity to our personal relationships, our health, and our overall well-being. We learn to enjoy the present more, to not obsess over what could have been, and to accept what is, with grace and equanimity.

In short, the philosophy of detachment is a powerful tool for any trader. It allows us to operate from a place of greater clarity, discipline, and emotional control. By letting go of attachment to immediate results, we free ourselves from the emotional roller coaster that trading can represent and focus on the long-term process. It helps us accept losses, let go of the need to control the market, and enjoy the ride itself more. And, most importantly, it gives us greater peace of mind, both in and out of the trading world.

Rituals for a Successful Trading Session

Rituals are a fundamental part of many people's daily lives. They help us structure our day, create a sense of purpose, and in many cases, increase our productivity. In the world of trading, where focus and discipline are key, establishing rituals can make a huge difference. Rituals for a successful trading session not only prepare our mind and body to face the market, but they also help us enter a state of calm and focus, which is crucial for making rational decisions and avoiding falling into emotional traps.

Before starting to trade, one of the most important rituals a trader can develop is to create a suitable environment. The environment in which we trade has a direct impact on our mental state. If we trade in a cluttered or distraction-filled space, chances are our mind is scattered as well. That's why the first step to a successful trading session is to make sure our workspace is clean, tidy, and free of unnecessary distractions. A clear desk and a quiet environment allow our mind to be clearer and ready to face the challenges of the market.

A very useful ritual before starting a trading session is to practice some form of meditation or conscious breathing. The market can be a very stressful place, and emotions can often cloud our judgment. Meditation, even for a few minutes, helps us calm the mind, reduce anxiety, and focus on the present. It's not about doing a deep meditation or spending hours in silence, but about taking a few minutes to focus on our breathing, letting go of any external worries, and bringing our full attention to the present moment. This simple ritual can make a huge difference in how we approach the trading day.

Another crucial aspect of rituals is setting clear goals for the session. Without goals, it's easy to get lost in the chaos of the market, make impulsive decisions, or deviate from the plan. Before we start trading, it's important to define what we want to achieve that day. These goals can be both financial and operational. Maybe our goal is to strictly follow our entry and exit strategy, or maybe we want to make sure we don't trade beyond a certain risk limit. By having clear goals, we know exactly what we're looking for and stay focused on our objectives throughout the session.

Once we have thought about and set our goals, it is useful to conduct a pre-market analysis. This involves reviewing what has happened in the markets prior to our session. There may have been important events, such as economic data announcements or global news, that could impact market behavior during our trading day. This pre-market analysis also helps us identify potential opportunities and risks. It allows us to enter the session with a clearer understanding of market conditions, which prepares us to make more informed decisions.

One ritual that many successful traders practice is to visualize their trades before they begin. Creative visualization doesn't just apply to sports or personal goals, but can also be a powerful tool in trading. Before we begin trading, we can take a few minutes to close our eyes and visualize a successful session. We can imagine how we analyze charts, how we make clear and precise decisions, how we stay calm during times of volatility, and how we follow our trading plan without deviating. By visualizing success, we are preparing our mind to trade from a place of confidence and focus.

It is also helpful to incorporate a strategy review ritual. Before we begin trading, it is important to remind ourselves of our trading plan. This includes our entry and exit criteria, our position sizes, and our risk limits. By reviewing our strategy before the action begins, we avoid making impulsive decisions or deviating from our plan due to the emotions of the moment. This ritual helps us maintain discipline and consistency in our decisions, two key elements for long-term success in trading.

During the trading session, it is important to maintain some small rituals that help us stay focused. For example, taking regular breaks to stretch or simply take a breath can be very beneficial. Trading requires a high level of mental focus, and trading for hours without a break can lead to mental exhaustion and avoidable mistakes. By scheduling small breaks throughout the session, we allow our mind to refresh, which helps us maintain a more sustained state of concentration.

In addition to breaks, a good ritual is to keep a real-time trading journal. During the session, we can record our trades, what we are seeing in the market, how we are feeling at certain times, and any adjustments we are considering making. Not only does this journal help us stay more aware of our decisions, but it also becomes a valuable tool to review at the end of the day. By writing down our trades in the moment, we are creating an honest and detailed record that we can later use to learn from our experiences, both positive and negative.

Once a trading session is over, it is important to have a closing ritual. This is a time to disconnect from the market and reflect on what has happened. We can review our trades, see what went well, what went wrong, and what we could improve. It is an opportunity to learn from our mistakes without being too self-critical, and also to celebrate the right decisions. This review ritual is key to continued growth as traders, as it allows us to adjust and fine-tune our strategy based on daily experiences.

Just like at the beginning of the session, meditation or conscious breathing can be helpful at the end of the day. After several hours of intense concentration and constant decision-making, it is normal to feel mentally exhausted. Ending the session with a few minutes of meditation allows us to release any accumulated tension and close the day with a sense of calm and clarity. This closing ritual helps us not to carry the stress of the market into other areas of our lives, which is crucial to maintaining a healthy balance between trading and personal well-being.

Finally, it is important to remember that rituals not only prepare us for a successful trading session, but they also help us build a mindset that is suitable for the long term. Trading is not an activity that is mastered overnight. It requires discipline, patience, and a constant focus on continuous improvement. By establishing daily rituals, we are creating a system that supports us on the path to success.

These rituals not only help us improve our technical skills, but they also allow us to take care of our mind and body, which is essential for optimal performance in any field.

In short, rituals for a successful trading session are essential to prepare our mind, body, and environment to face the market with clarity and focus. From meditation before we begin, to visualizing our trades, to reviewing at the end of the day, these rituals give us a structure and a solid foundation to operate from a place of calm and confidence. They help us maintain discipline, avoid emotional decisions, and continually learn from our experiences. Incorporating rituals into our daily routine as traders will not only make us more effective in the market, but will also allow us to enjoy the process more and maintain a healthy balance between work and personal well-being.

Trading as a Path to Personal Growth

Trading is much more than just a financial activity or a way to make money in the markets. For those who truly delve into this world, trading becomes a path of personal growth. Through the ups and downs, the wins and losses, we are confronted not only with market fluctuations, but also with our own emotions, beliefs and behaviors. Every trade, every market session is an opportunity to learn something new about ourselves, about how we react under pressure, about our strengths and, of course, our weaknesses. Trading, like any path of growth, challenges us to become better, more aware and more disciplined in all aspects of our lives.

One of the first challenges that trading presents us with is the need to learn to manage our emotions. Fear, greed, euphoria and frustration are emotions that every trader experiences at some point. When we see a trade go against us, we feel the fear of losing money. When we win, euphoria can lead us to risk more than we should in the next trade. In this sense, trading is like a mirror that reflects our deepest emotions, and learning to manage them is an essential lesson in this path of personal growth. By working on emotional control, we not only become better traders, but also more balanced and conscious people in our daily lives.

Trading also teaches us about the importance of discipline. It is often said that success in trading is not so much based on the ability to predict the market, but on the ability to follow a strategy in a consistent and disciplined manner. Many traders have a solid strategy, but fail to follow through on emotions or by not following their own plans. Discipline is what allows us to stick to our strategy, even when the market seems to be against us. This type of self-discipline is a skill that transcends the world of trading and applies to all areas of life. Whether it is in our personal relationships, our work, or our long-term goals, discipline is what allows us to keep going when things get tough.

Another aspect of personal growth that trading offers us is the ability to learn from our mistakes. In trading, making mistakes is inevitable. No matter how much experience or knowledge we have, there will always be times when we make wrong decisions. The key is not to avoid mistakes, but to learn from them. Every losing trade is a lesson in disguise, an opportunity to analyze what went wrong and adjust our strategy. This approach of constant learning is critical not only in trading, but in life in general. By developing the humility to accept our mistakes and the curiosity to learn from them, we become more resilient and adaptable people, capable of facing any challenge that comes our way.

Trading also teaches us about patience. In a world where many things happen quickly and where we are taught to seek instant gratification, trading reminds us that some of the best opportunities take time. Not every trade will happen right away, and many times we will have to wait for the market to align with our strategy. This patience, which is crucial to success in trading, is also a valuable lesson for life. Learning to wait, not to rush, and to trust the process is a skill that helps us manage the uncertainties and complexities we face in our daily lives.

One of the most profound aspects of trading as a path to personal growth is that it leads us to get to know ourselves better. When we are trading, we are faced not only with the market, but also with our own fears, desires and expectations. Trading forces us to be honest with ourselves, to recognize our weaknesses and to work on them. If we are impatient, trading will reveal it. If we are overconfident or constantly doubt our decisions, the market will let us know. This forced introspection gives us the opportunity to grow as individuals, to recognize our behavioral patterns and to make the necessary changes to improve, not only in trading, but in our lives in general.

Trading also teaches us about detachment, a fundamental lesson for emotional well-being. In trading, we must learn to detach ourselves from individual outcomes. Each trade is just a small part of a much bigger picture. There will be winning trades and there will be losing trades, and neither of them define our long-term success. This detachment is not only crucial in trading, but also in life. By learning to let go of the need to control every outcome, we free ourselves from unnecessary pressure and stress. We become more flexible, more adaptable, and more able to enjoy the process, rather than being obsessed with the end result.

A key component of personal growth in trading is humility. The market has a unique way of keeping us humble. No matter how successful a trading streak is, there will always be times when the market surprises us or shows us that we don't have all the answers. This humility is what keeps us constantly learning. It reminds us that there is always more to learn, that we can always improve, and that the market is bigger than any individual trader. Humility is what allows us to keep moving forward after a loss and what keeps us focused on learning and growing, rather than being driven by ego.

Another interesting aspect of trading as a path to personal growth is that it teaches us to embrace uncertainty. In the market, we never have guarantees. No matter how well we analyze a situation or how confident we are about a trade, there is always the possibility that things will not turn out the way we expect. This acceptance of uncertainty is a valuable lesson for life. Often, we try to control every aspect of our lives, seeking certainty and security in a world that is, by nature, uncertain. Trading teaches us to be comfortable with the unknown, to accept that we will not always have all the answers, and to trust in our ability to adapt to any situation.

Finally, trading offers us the opportunity to develop a growth mindset. Instead of seeing success or failure as fixed, trading invites us to adopt the mindset that we can always improve. Every day, every market session is an opportunity to learn something new, to refine our strategy, to improve our ability to make decisions under pressure. This growth mindset is key not only to success in trading, but to any aspect of life. It allows us to face challenges with curiosity and openness, rather than with fear or resignation. It teaches us that, with the right amount of time and effort, we can always improve.

In short, trading is much more than a financial activity. For those who are willing to dive into this world with the right mindset, trading becomes a true path of personal growth. Through managing our emotions, developing discipline, accepting our mistakes, and practicing patience and detachment, trading challenges us to become better, not just as traders, but as individuals. It teaches us to know ourselves on a deeper level, to embrace uncertainty, and to adopt a growth mindset. In this sense, true success in trading is not measured only by financial gains, but by the personal evolution we experience along the way.

www.ingramcontent.com/pod-product-compliance
Lightning Source LLC
Chambersburg PA
CBHW051855130726
47987CB00002B/847